Timothy Whuffenpuffen-Whippersnapper

Written by Sally Odgers
Illustrated by John Bennett

© 1995 Shortland Publications Limited

00 99 98 97 96

10 9 8 7 6 5 4 3 2

Published by Shortland Publications Limited, 2B Cawley St, Ellerslie, Auckland, New Zealand.

Distributed in the United States of America by

a division of Reed Elsevier Inc.
500 Coventry Lane
Crystal Lake, IL 60014
800-822-8661

Distributed in Canada by

PRENTICE HALL GINN
1870 Birchmount Road
Scarborough
Ontario M1P 2J7

Printed through Bookbuilders Limited, Hong Kong

ISBN: 0-7901-0988-3

Contents

CHAPTER ONE

In Which
Marcus Receives
a Squirming Parcel

The postman had delivered a letter and a brown paper parcel. The parcel was squirming, so it was probably an Amazonian python, or something worse.

Marcus swallowed, and called out to Mom. "Hey, Mom! I've got a parcel!"

Mom came in from the kitchen. She sighed, because Marcus always reminded her of a frightened rabbit. "It's probably your Christmas present from your Great Uncle Hinkley," she said briskly, picking up the letter. "I can't think of what else it could possibly be." She sighed again. "Oh dear, I do wish Hinkley wouldn't do it."

"Wouldn't do what? Send me presents?"

"I wish he wouldn't send you presents that

are alive," said Mom. "It's such a nuisance, and I really do hate having to take them all to the zoo."

Marcus looked suspiciously at the parcel. It wasn't squirming now. Maybe it wasn't a python, after all.

Mom and Marcus had never actually met Great Uncle Hinkley, but they knew what he looked like from a framed portrait that hung above the fireplace. The portrait had been painted in oils by a famous artist named Euphemia Haycock many years before. It showed a very young, red-haired Great Uncle Hinkley, wearing ridiculous checked pants with blue suspenders, and a big grin. Apart from the pants and the grin, he looked just like Marcus. The painting was valuable, which was rather a pity, because that meant it had to be insured.

"I wish I could have sold it to that woman who wanted to buy it last month," said Mom longingly. "The one with the funny name, who asked all the peculiar questions. Petrocelli or something. She seemed to think we knew someone called Timothy... But it wouldn't have been the right thing to do. Not while the old gentleman keeps sending you expensive presents every Christmas. I suppose it isn't his fault we can never keep them."

The presents caused a lot of trouble. Marcus and Mom lived in a flat on the third floor of Blankstone Buildings.

```
┌─────────────────────────────────────┐
│                                      │
│     RULES FOR TENANTS                │
│       OF BLANKSTONE                  │
│         BUILDINGS                    │
│                                      │
│       No noise. No music.            │
│    No fires in the courtyard.        │
│          No complaints.              │
│          And strictly                │
│                                      │
│     NO PETS ALLOWED.                 │
│                                      │
│  BY ORDER — R. MEANER — LANDLORD     │
│                                      │
└─────────────────────────────────────┘
```

Great Uncle Hinkley, on the other hand, lived in a caravan, traveling all over the world with his Circus of Wonder. They never knew quite from where the next letter would come. They had received postcards from Port

Douglas, from The Alice, from Wellington, and Kathmandu, and once a card had come from Antarctica. A pet penguin had followed by mail, but Mom had sent the penguin to the zoo. She had sent the llama from Kathmandu and the turtle from Port Douglas to the zoo as well, and even the frilled lizard from The Alice.

The kiwi from Wellington hadn't been a problem. It had never even arrived, because it had been repossessed at the airport by a naturalist. That was just as well, because it would have had to go to the zoo with the others. Mom hated sending away Great Uncle Hinkley's presents, but she had no choice.

"What does the letter say?" asked Marcus. He didn't want to open the parcel yet, in case it was a python.

Mom unfolded two sheets of paper. "That's odd," she said after a moment. "There seems to be two letters here."

"Maybe he's sent next year's as well," said Marcus, but Mom was shaking her head. "Oh dear," she said, reading the shorter letter. "Oh, the poor old man." And she read the letter aloud.

McDAFTIE, McDAFTIE, AND McDAFTIE
SOLICITORS AND TRUSTEES SINCE 1605

December 29

Mrs. Veronica Whippersnapper
Flat 16, Blankstone Buildings

Dear Madam,

For some years, we have acted as solicitors
and trustees for our client, Mr. Hinkley Q.
Whippersnapper. Now as per instructions, we
are carrying out his wishes in sending the
accompanying legacy to your son, Marcus
Whippersnapper.

The enclosed letter to your son from our
client will, I trust, more fully explain
matters.

Yours faithfully,

Fergus McDaftie

Fergus McDaftie

"Does that mean Great Uncle Hinkley's
dead, then?" asked Marcus.

"I suppose so," said Mom. "A legacy is a
gift left in a will. I wonder what happened to
the Circus of Wonder." She handed the other
letter to Marcus.

Marcus read the letter aloud.

My Dear Marcus,

Although we've never met, I feel I know a lot about you. I know that you are a true Whippersnapper, with blue eyes and red hair. I know you are eleven years old, and I know that you live with your mother, widow of my much-beloved (though seldom encountered) nephew Narrington Whippersnapper. I have often toyed with the idea of retiring and coming to live with you and your dear mother, but this, I fear, is not to be.

When you read this letter, you will know that I have gone to a better place (that is, if that old fool Fergus McDaftie obeys his instructions!). This being the case, I am sending you a small heirloom that has been in the Whippersnapper family for generations. Had I a son, it would pass to him. In the circumstances, it must now come to you ~ last of the line ~ to prepare you for your destiny.

I trust that when the time comes you will pass it on to a son of your own.

Your affectionate

Great Uncle Hinkley

10

"The poor old man," Mom said again. "But I must admit he was peculiar. A letter a year for the past eleven years isn't much contact. And if he'd only bothered to read the letters I sent him, he'd have known not to keep sending you all those pets. Still – it seems he's sent you a nice keepsake, though I don't know what he means about destiny."

"Wh-what do you reckon it is this time, Mom?" Marcus prodded the parcel gently with his ruler. "Do you reckon it's a p-python?"

"Goodness knows," said Mom. "I doubt it. The parcel isn't jumping up and down for once. Some sort of circus trick, or maybe an antique clown costume. You'd like that, wouldn't you? You could wear it to the school dance."

"I'm not going to the school dance," said Marcus.

"Oh, Marcus! Why ever not?"

"Amanda Barton-Boote will be there, and she'll want to make me dance."

"Oh," said Mom. "Maybe Amanda would like to wear the clown costume, then."

Marcus prodded the parcel again. "I don't think it's a clown costume," he said in a doom-laden voice. I think it's a python."

"Only one way to find out," said Mom briskly. "Unwrap it and see."

"Can't you?" asked Marcus, but Mom gave him a look, so he cut the string and pulled apart the paper.

"Thank goodness for that!" remarked the contents of the parcel as the waxed paper fell away. "I was somewhat tired of holding my breath."

Mom and Marcus stared at what had been in the parcel. "What is it?" said Mom.

"Well," said Marcus doubtfully, "I'm not sure, but I think it's a dragon."

CHAPTER TWO

In Which
Timothy Whuffenpuffen
Recounts His History

"Of course I'm a dragon," said the dragon. It shook itself until its scales rattled and ruffled its gleaming wings. "What else?"

"Oh dear," said Mom. "Another donation to the zoo."

"But he's only a little dragon," said Marcus. "Not much bigger than a cat."

Mom was surprised he hadn't backed away. "Size has nothing to do with it," she said. "You can't keep a dragon in any flat, let alone Blankstone Buildings. If Mr. Meaner clapped his eyes on this fellow, he'd have us out before you could say boo! Besides, it *is* a dragon."

The dragon squirted a little jet of flame, and this time Marcus *did* jump back.

"Pardon me," remarked the dragon, looking

at Marcus. "As I informed you, I have been holding my breath, and this is hard on us dragons." Its eyes were jewel-blue and shone like chips of sapphire. "You, young sir, I apprehend you are my new Master Whippersnapper?"

"No!" said Mom.

"Yes, I am," said Marcus. "At least, I think I would like to be. That is, if it wasn't for Mr. Meaner." His voice trailed off miserably. This dragon was the most splendid thing that had ever happened to him, but he knew it would have to go to the zoo, just like the penguin and the llama. Mr. Meaner would throw them out of the flat if they kept the dragon.

"Hey! What's burning?" said a voice, and Amanda Barton-Boote marched in, as usual, without knocking.

Amanda lived in the house down the road, and Marcus didn't like her much. She was very bossy, and she always thought she knew everything. Worse still, she had the horrible habit of dragging him along by the wrist, as if he was a rag doll. Worst of all, she wasn't a bit frightened of Zack Meaner, the landlord's son.

"Nothing's burning," said Marcus, glaring at Amanda.

"I can smell something," insisted Amanda, glaring back.

"It's only the dragon. *My* dragon." He thought he'd better make that clear right from the start.

"Gee," said Amanda, staring. "It really *is* a dragon! You *lucky* thing! What's its name?"

The dragon rattled its scales again. "Timothy Whuffenpuffen-Whippersnapper at your service," it said, with a bow of its crested head. "Got any fires you want lit? Got any sausages you want cooked? Got any enemies you want singed?"

"Lots!" said Amanda gleefully. "Let's go!"

"I'm so sorry," interrupted Mom, "but you can't stay here, Timothy. Pets are not allowed in Blankstone Buildings."

"But, Mom!" wailed Marcus.

"I have to go to work now, Marcus," interrupted Mom. "When I get home, we'll have to take Timothy to the zoo. No – don't argue. He'll be well looked after, just like all the others."

Mom hurried out so Marcus wouldn't see how much she hated saying he couldn't keep his dragon. It had been bad enough with the penguin, the llama, and the frilled lizard, but at least they hadn't been able to talk. Timothy was such a polite dragon, too, and so friendly. Marcus needed a friend. But what couldn't be couldn't be, and there was nothing she could do about it.

"I've got an idea," said Amanda, after a miserable pause.

"You would have," grumped Marcus. He felt like crying.

"He can come and live with me," said Amanda. "You'd like that, wouldn't you Timothy Whuffenpuffen? We've got a nice, big yard, and even a barbecue."

Marcus didn't want Amanda to have his dragon, but at least it would be better than sending poor Timothy Whuffenpuffen to the zoo. "Yes," he said in a rush. "You take him, Amanda. Just remember he really belongs to me."

"Come on, Timothy," said Amanda. "Will you walk, or shall I carry you? Do I need asbestos gloves?"

The dragon backed away. "Excuse me, Missamanda," it said politely, "but I cannot live with you."

"Why not?" said Amanda. "Marcus can't

keep you here – old Meaner won't allow it. So it's me or the zoo. I'm not big-headed, but I know which one I'd choose."

"You, Missamanda, are not, I'm afraid, a Whippersnapper," said Timothy, still politely.

"Huh?"

"You're a Barton-Boote," muttered Marcus.

"So?" bristled Amanda. "Barton-Bootes are as good as Whippersnappers, anytime."

Timothy coughed. "It is engraved upon my contract," he said, "that I must live with a flame-haired scion of the Whippersnappers. It is engraved in mingled blood."

"Blood!" Even Amanda looked appalled. "Whose blood?"

"Mine," said the dragon. "My blood and that of my Master Whippersnapper. My first Master Whippersnapper, that is. Master Horatio."

"Who'd want to sign a contract in blood?" said Amanda. "I mean, that's really gross."

The dragon sighed. "I see I must recount my history," he said. "Then you may understand." And he began.

"Many years ago, there was a far-off country we dragons called Dragonreign."

"Never heard of it," said Amanda.

The dragon ignored her and continued. "We dragon folk were happy and prosperous, building nests, rearing young, harming no one except the odd rabbit. Humans came occasionally to our land, but we avoided them wherever possible, as few were kindly disposed to us. Then, there came a man who was different, a man who intruded upon our notice and invited our friendship. A man with hair as red as dragon fire. Just like your hair, Master Whippersnapper."

"What was his name?" asked Marcus. "And will you stop calling me Master Whippersnapper? Call me Marcus."

"His name, Master Marcus," said the dragon, "was Whippersnapper – Horatio Pegleg Whippersnapper. He was a sea captain, whose ship had gone down just off the rocks of Dragon Bay.

"Horatio Whippersnapper was a bold, brave man, and he swam ashore to Dragonreign. We dragons knew him for a hero from the start. We treated him well, but he wished to return to his own land, where he was promised in marriage to a certain young lady. His ship was wrecked, so we dragons decided to help him get home. We drew lots for the honor, and when the time came, I was chosen."

"How could you help him?" asked Marcus.

Timothy looked offended. "I, Master Marcus, am as able as any other dragon! I had taken a fancy to Master Horatio, so I conducted him on his journey. We returned to his homeland, where he married the young lady (her name was Bonny Lucy, by the way). In due course, a child was born. Master Horatio decided to sail away again in search of treasure. Before he left, he charged me with the safekeeping of his son, Master Horribald."

There was a splutter from Amanda. "Horribald? Horribald? What sort of a name is that?"

"A fine name," said the dragon. "We drew up a contract in blood, and each signed his mark, and when Master Horatio sailed away, I remained behind with my new Master Whippersnapper, Master Horribald. I served him faithfully for seventy years. When he died, I was bequeathed to his son, a sprightly young man of forty-five. His name was Hoffenbach. I served Master Hoffenbach for twenty-five years, and was again bequeathed, this time to a grandson named Hemlock. I served him for..."

"Timothy," said Marcus, "just how many Master Whippersnappers have you had?"

The jewel-blue eyes rolled thoughtfully. "Counting you, Master Marcus, I believe the number to be upward of forty. The Whippersnappers are a long-lived breed."

"And have you never wanted to go back to Dragonreign?"

"Not while there remains a scion of the Whippersnappers for me to serve."

Marcus and Amanda stared. "You must be awfully old, Timothy!" said Amanda.

The dragon shrugged. "Perhaps I am, Missamanda, but there's a saying: A dragon is only as old as he feels. Besides – my contract has given me reason to go on."

"And your contract says you have to live with a Whippersnapper," said Amanda. "And the contract is signed in blood."

"Correct," said Timothy. "The actual contract was lost long ago, but its intention remains."

Marcus frowned. Mom couldn't expect him to break a contract signed in *blood*, could she? No, but Mr. Meaner could. Mr. Meaner *would*. "You can't go to the zoo, then," he said, "not if you've got to live with me. But you can't stay here either."

"I see," said the dragon.

"You'll *have* to live with me," said Amanda. "Marcus can visit you every day."

"Unfortunately," said Timothy, "a broken contract means a dead dragon. However, one must resign oneself to the inevitable." And he visibly did so.

CHAPTER THREE

In Which
Timothy Whuffenpuffen
Grows – and Shrinks

"That's it, then," said Amanda. "We can't let him die. Not after he's served all those Whippersnapper Masters."

"But I can't keep him!" wailed Marcus. "Mom won't let me!"

"For heaven's sake!" said Amanda. "Don't be such a wimp. If you can't keep him here, you'll have to move to a place where you *can* keep him."

Marcus sighed. "Do you think we *like* living here? The thing is, we *have* to live here, Amanda. The lease is for ten years. My dad signed it just before he died, and by the time Mom found out, it was too late. She won't break a lease."

"She will if you make her."

"How?"

"Easy," said Amanda. "You can *run away*."

"I can't."

"Yes you can. Take Timothy Whuffenpuffen and go. Write your mom a note and say you'll come home only if you can keep Timothy. After all," said Amanda solemnly, "it's a matter of life and death!"

Marcus bit his lip. "I can see that," he said, "but where could we go?"

Amanda rolled her eyes. Really, Marcus *was* hopeless. If Timothy had been *her* dragon, she would have known exactly what to do. But then, she didn't live in Blankstone Buildings.

"Go and hide in the school," she said. "It's all shut up for the holidays, so you can stay there for weeks. Go on, Marcus, it's got everything – showers, bathrooms, even a kitchen. And there's a cot in the nurse's office."

"Oh, all right," said Marcus. "But how do I get in?"

"Do I have to think of everything?" said Amanda. "You can get in through the window in the girls' bathroom. The latch doesn't work. Take your bike." She leaned back and folded her arms. "Anything else you need to know?"

"Yes," said Marcus unhappily. "How am I going to get past Zack?"

"Wimp," said Amanda.

Marcus blushed and went to fetch his backpack. He put some cans of food in it, and wrote a note to his mother.

Dear Mum,
I'm running away because I've got to keep Timothy Whuffenpuffen. His contract says he'll die if he has to go to the zoo or live with Amanda. I'll come back when you say I can keep him. Amanda knows where I am. She won't tell you, but she'll tell me when you make up your mind.
love, Marcus

"That'll bring her around," said Amanda, reading over his shoulder.

Marcus turned to Timothy. "If you can get in this bag," he said, "I can carry you downstairs. Keep quiet. I don't want Zack Meaner to hear us. He keeps threatening to take my bike."

"I'll give the note to your mom," said Amanda.

Marcus crept out of the flat and down the stairs. He was out of luck; there was Zack Meaner, hanging over the stair railing like a gorilla from a banana tree.

"Hey, Whippersnapper!" he yelled. "About that bike!"

Marcus began to run, but Zack dropped down and followed him. Marcus reached the place where he kept his bike first. It was a new bike, a Christmas present from Mom, and Marcus kept it locked to the railing in the courtyard. Zack caught up while he was still trying to undo the padlock.

"I *said*, what about that bike?" said Zack, breathing down the back of his neck.

"No, I won't," gasped Marcus. "You'll only smash it up, like you did yours."

"Yeah, I will," said Zack. "Then we'll be even, won't we, Whippersnapper? Why should you have a bike when I don't?" He picked up a brick from the corner of the courtyard.

"Don't!" cried Marcus, but Zack had already heaved the brick at the bike.

The spokes of the back wheel twanged, but didn't break. Zack began to kick at the tires. He was wearing heavy boots with steel tips, so the bike bounced with every kick.

"Stop that!" yelled Marcus, but Zack shoved him away.

"Pardon me," said a voice politely from

inside the backpack, "but may I be of service, Master Marcus?"

"Ssh!" hissed Marcus. He grabbed for the pack, but the zipper was already creeping back. Timothy Whuffenpuffen-Whippersnapper poked his head out of the bag. "Misguided youth, cease this attempt to damage my master's property," he told Zack.

"Yeah? Says who?" panted Zack, trying to twist the handlebars out of shape.

"Says I, Timothy Whuffenpuffen-Whippersnapper," said the dragon.

Zack glanced at the backpack and guffawed. "A puppet! Really, Whippersnapper, you're such a baby!"

"I am not a puppet. I am a dragon," stated Timothy. "Kindly stand back, Master Marcus, while I deal with this ungracious person."

"No, don't!" cried Marcus. "He'll do something horrible to you!"

"On the contrary," said Timothy. "I shall do something horrible to *him*." He stepped out of the bag and drew in a deep breath. "I shall grow," he announced, and he grew.

And grew.

Within two seconds, he towered over both boys.

Within four seconds, his crested head brushed the windowsill of the second-floor flat.

He reached out a front foot the size of a wheelbarrow, and fit the claws around Zack's waist. Neatly, Timothy plucked Zack away from the bike.

Zack screamed, and fainted.

"What do you wish me to do with this misguided person now, Master Marcus?" asked Timothy. His precise voice sounded ridiculous coming from such a huge dragon.

"Put him down!" cried Marcus, staring at the dangling Zack.

The dragon nodded. "Certainly, if that is your wish, Master Marcus." He draped Zack carefully over the trash cans in the corner. "Fear not, he is quite unhurt."

"What's going on?" cried Amanda, from the window above. "Wow!" She ran out of the flat, slid down the banister, and came out into the courtyard to stare with popping eyes at the dragon. "What...?" she said.

"Stop it!" yelled Marcus. "Stop it at once!"

Timothy bent his head. "Do I take it, Master Marcus, that you wish me to resume my former proportions?"

"Yes, yes, resume!" said Marcus. "I can't carry you like that!"

Timothy began to shrink. "What size would you like me to be, Master Marcus?" he asked, as his head dropped below the second-floor window.

"Your normal size, of course!"

"Alas," said Timothy, as he dropped below shoulder height. "I have no normal size. It is a matter of what you wish. Master Hinkley preferred me the same size as his pet cat. He said it saved trouble."

"You mean you can be any size at all?" Amanda asked eagerly. "Any size you want?"

"Any size my Master Marcus wants," corrected Timothy. By now he was cat-sized, and still shrinking.

Marcus considered. "Could you get small enough to fit in – say – a matchbox?" he asked.

"No trouble at all!" Timothy shrank again. "Is this what you had in mind, Master Marcus?"

Marcus bent down and picked up his dragon, now a mere two centimeters tall. "Can you stay like this?" he asked.

"I shall remain this size until you desire me to change," promised Timothy.

Amanda let out a big breath. "We can keep him!" she burst out. "He'd be easy to hide, and he won't take up any room... No one will know we've got him at all!"

"*I've* got him," corrected Marcus. "Not *we*."

"Quite so," remarked the dragon.

"Can't I help you?" asked Amanda. "Please?"

Marcus stared. Amanda Barton-Boote saying "please?" To him? Amazing!

"If you like," he said grandly.

Zack stirred and opened his eyes. "Wha – wha – help! Don't let it get me!" he wailed, looking around wildly.

"Don't let *what* get you?" asked Amanda innocently.

"It! The thing! The monster!"

Amanda smiled, not very nicely. "I can't see any monster," she said. "Do you see any monster, Marcus?"

"No," said Marcus, closing his hand gently over Timothy Whuffenpuffen-Whippersnapper. "I don't see any monster at all. By the way,

Zack, do you still want to smash my bike?"

But Zack was already running upstairs to his flat.

"That got rid of *him*!" said Amanda with satisfaction. "He won't bother you after this."

But she was wrong.

When he wasn't looking for someone to bully, Zack spent most of his time watching videos and eating pizza and drinking brightly colored cordial. By lunchtime the next day, he had talked himself into believing Timothy was a nightmare, brought on by too many horror movies and too much cheese.

CHAPTER FOUR

In Which
Zack Meaner Is
Slightly Singed

Mom came home cross and tired. "Where is he?" she said, looking around the flat.

"Where's who?" asked Marcus.

"That dragon."

Marcus reached into his pocket and pulled out Timothy. "I can keep him now, can't I?" he said.

Mom peered in astonishment. "Is that the same dragon?" she asked.

Marcus nodded.

"But how can it be? It's tiny."

"Show her, Timothy," said Marcus.

So Timothy grew until he was as high as the table, and then shrank down to matchbox height once more. "See Mom?" said Marcus eagerly. "He can be any size he wants. *Now* can

I keep him? He's got a contract that says he'll die if he doesn't live with me."

Mom hesitated, then nodded. "Yes, all right, under the circumstances. As long as Mr. Meaner doesn't find out."

"I promise, I absolutely *promise* I'll never let that happen," said Marcus.

Mom smiled. "Welcome to your new home, Timothy!"

"Thank you, Madam." Timothy looked around the shabby room, with its uneven doorstep and chipped furniture, and spotted the painting above the fireplace. "What a fine portrait of Master Hinkley," he observed.

"I suppose it is," said Mom. "Oddly enough, someone offered to buy it only last week. A Miss Pepperoni or some such name. I might sell it if she comes back. If you've no objection."

"I have no objection," said Timothy, "but perhaps Master Hinkley might wish to be *consulted*."

Mom and Marcus stared. "Great Uncle Hinkley is dead," said Mom.

"He is not," said Timothy.

"Well – he must be," said Marcus. "He sent you to live with me."

"And in the letter he says – where is it?" said Mom. She picked up the letter from Great Uncle Hinkley. "Yes. He says... *I cannot know precisely when you will read this letter, but when you do read it, you will know that I have gone to a better place.'* She folded the letter. "So you see, Timothy, he must be dead."

"I beg your pardon, Madam," said Timothy, "but I must point out that Master Hinkley says merely that he has *gone to a better place*. He makes no mention of death."

Mom shook her head. "But that's what he *meant*. Everyone knows that *'gone to a better place'* means *'dead.'* It's just a softer way of putting it."

"Not with Master Hinkley," said Timothy stubbornly. "If Master Hinkley meant 'dead,' he would have said 'dead.' Master Hinkley has no use for soft ways of saying things."

"Then what can he mean?" asked Mom. "And why did he send you here?"

"I suspect," said Timothy, "he means that he has gone to a better place than Meadow-upon-Woad. And perhaps he felt Master Marcus was more in need of my services than he."

"But where *is* Uncle Hinkley?"

"As to that," said the dragon, "I have no idea. He did not inform me of his plans."

"What was wrong with Chigwell Drive? It sounds like a respectable address to me," said Mom.

"It is not my place to speculate," said Timothy, "but perhaps Master Hinkley was troubled by the Flying Gonzaloonies. They have been somewhat unsettled of late, and when unsettled, they tend to be garrulous. Is it your wish that I set out with Master Marcus to search for Master Hinkley, Madam? We could then consult him as to his wishes regarding the portrait."

"No!" said Mom. "I mean, no thank you, Timothy. I don't have the buyer's address, so there's no point. And Timothy, I think you'll just have to accept the fact that Uncle Hinkley may be dead."

"Oh, no," said Timothy. "My Master Hinkley would never have been so impolite as to die without telling me. It would be most unworthy of a Whippersnapper."

"I see," said Mom slowly. "Your Master Hinkley is a polite person, is he?"

But Timothy had suddenly become very

busy in cleaning his crest and did not answer.

The next week was the best Marcus could remember. Amanda Barton-Boote came over rather often, but for once, Marcus felt equal to dealing with her. After all, he was a flame-haired scion of the Whippersnappers. She was only a Barton-Boote.

Most of the time, Timothy remained matchbox sized. It was more convenient for all of them, especially Marcus, who had to keep him out of Mr. Meaner's sight. Timothy's voice sounded the same whatever size he was, and his one-centimeter flames were unlikely to set anything on fire, so he was easy to look after, eating almost anything and snoozing in an old baking dish lined with tinfoil and pigeon feathers. Carrying him around was no problem either – he fit nicely into a pocket. It was so simple that one wet day they got careless.

The rain was streaming down, and Marcus and Amanda were in the flat preparing to cook sausages for lunch. Amanda was insisting they should go for a walk afterward. Marcus was telling her it was too wet.

"These sausages would be a lot nicer if they were grilled," said Amanda. "Fried sausages are unhealthy."

"The grill's broken," said Marcus.

"What about Timothy Whuffenpuffen? Timothy, do you think you could barbecue some sausages for us?"

"Certainly, Missamanda," said Timothy. "If Master Marcus wishes."

Marcus hesitated. Amanda was being bossy again, but the sausages *would* be nicer if they were brown and crisp, instead of damp and fatty. "All right," he said. "But we'd better go outside. Mom won't like it if we get smoke marks on the ceiling."

"We'll go in the courtyard," said Amanda. "Timothy will have to make himself a bit bigger, otherwise his flame won't be enough."

They were happily barbecuing sausages when Zack, attracted by the smell of cooking, poked his head out the door. Sausages! Mmm! Zack decided to go and take some.

They'd make a nice change from pizza, and besides, they belonged to someone else.

That was always a good enough reason for Zack Meaner.

Following the scent, he came down the steps into the courtyard, and there, tucked away in a corner, were Marcus Whippersnapper and Amanda Barton-Boote. They were crouched over, as if they were examining something on the ground – or cooking over a campfire.

"A bit more on this side, Timothy," he heard the bossy Barton-Boote girl say. Giving orders as usual, but to whom? Wimpy Whippersnapper's name was Marcus, not Timothy.

A puff of sausage-scented smoke tickled Zack's nose, and he sniffed hungrily. Cooking in the courtyard was against the rules. Zack crept a little closer, then he sprang.

"Got you!" he howled, grabbing Marcus by the shoulder. Marcus pulled away, and Zack lost his balance, knocking the two of them to the ground. There was a quick scuttling sound, a squeak, and then silence. Zack used Marcus's shoulder to push himself up. "Now look what you've made me do!" he yelped. "I've got ketchup all over my shirt! My dad'll kill you!"

"It's your fault," said Marcus. "You pushed me over."

Zack stared. "You're very brave all of a sudden," he said, poking Marcus in the chest with one finger.

Behind him, Amanda laughed. "You weren't so brave yourself last week, Zack Meaner!"

"What d'you mean?"

"She doesn't mean anything," said Marcus loudly. "Nothing at all. Go away, Zack. We're not doing anything."

Zack's eyes narrowed. "You were cooking," he said. "And you've got some sort of animal in your pocket. I can see it moving. Give it here, and I'll wring its neck." Holding Marcus by the collar, Zack reached out and seized Timothy.

"Blimey!" he said, and stared at the dangling dragon. But not for long. In a moment, he yelled and let go.

Marcus grabbed Timothy. "I think we'd better go inside," he gabbled, and for once, Amanda agreed.

"I'll get you for this, Whippersnapper!" yelled Zack, sucking his fingers.

"What did you do to him, Timothy?" asked Marcus when they were safely in the flat.

Timothy coughed. "Your pardon, Master Marcus, but I singed his fingers. Only very slightly; he will have sustained no lasting injury – except to his pride. I regret the necessity, but it seemed sensible to effect a speedy escape."

"That's all right, then," said Amanda.

But it wasn't.

CHAPTER FIVE

In Which Zack Meaner Gets His Revenge, and the Whippersnappers Are Evicted

The first thing Zack Meaner did was hold his scorched fingers under the cold tap. The water poured down the drain, and the pipes began to bang like a kindergarten music lesson.

The pipes in Blankstone Buildings were always banging, mostly because Mr. Meaner never had the plumbing fixed. The tenants' leases said the plumbing had to work, not that it had to be quiet, and Mr. Meaner always stuck to the letter of the law.

"Turn that water off!" yelled Mr. Meaner from the living room, where he was watching the television.

"I need it!" whined Zack. "That wimpy Whippersnapper kid, Marcus, made me burn my fingers!"

Mr. Meaner heaved himself out of his chair and marched into the kitchen. "Show me," he ordered, grabbing Zack's hand and leaning down to look. "Huh. Not much damage there. I s'pose you've been messing around with matches again. How many times have I told you..."

"It wasn't my fault!" said Zack. He scowled down at his fingers, noticing with annoyance that his dad was right: the redness was fading already. "It was that Marcus Whippersnapper," he said. "He and his stupid pet."

Mr. Meaner stiffened like a pointer on the scent of game. His nose, which was long and shaped like an arrowhead, quivered. "Pet?" he said. "What pet? Does that Whippersnapper child have a pet?"

Zack licked his lips. He hadn't really meant to tell his dad about Marcus's pet. Not because it would get Marcus into trouble, but because Zack had been looking forward to a nice session of blackmail. For example, he could have made Marcus give up his bike and some treats from his lunch box, and probably a lot of other things as well. Now that chance was gone.

"The pet," insisted Mr. Meaner, "tell me about the pet. Is it a dog? Surely it isn't a dog. I'd have been sneezing by now if it was."

He blew his nose at the thought.

Zack chewed his lip. "I didn't really mean to tell you," he said.

"Maybe not, but you might as well finish now that you've started. A cat is it? Or a bird?"

Zack shook his head. "It – it's a sort of lizard," he invented. "Or maybe a snake. Yes, that's what it might be. A snake."

"Right, that does it," said Mr. Meaner, putting away his handkerchief. "Remind me this evening, Zachary. I must pay a call on Mrs.

Veronica Whippersnapper."

Zack slouched back out to the courtyard and kicked at the brick wall. "Me and my big mouth," he muttered.

In flat 16, Marcus and Amanda were arguing.

"It's all your fault," said Marcus. "You wanted to have a barbecue."

"All right, die of a heart attack from fatty food!" snapped Amanda. "See if I care!" She scowled. "D'you reckon he saw Timothy?"

"Of course he saw Timothy," said Marcus miserably. "He had him in his horrible hand."

"And Timothy fixed him once and for all," said Amanda. "Great!" But she didn't sound very certain.

Amanda had to go home at four o'clock, and Mom came back from work at a quarter-past five. As usual, she looked weary, but she smiled at Marcus and Timothy. Marcus bit his lip and smiled back. He couldn't bring himself to tell her what had happened. Not after the promise he had made.

At half-past five precisely, there was a

knock on the door. "Bother," said Mom. "Just when I wanted to put my feet up. Go and see who it is, Marcus."

Marcus was afraid he already knew the answer to that, so he hid Timothy under the couch and opened the door. Outside were Mr. Meaner and Zack. Without waiting for an invitation, they came into the flat.

Mom closed her eyes for a second, then managed a cool smile. "What can I do for you today, Mr. Meaner?"

The landlord's nose twitched like a metal detector on the scent of gold. "I believe your son has acquired a pet lizard," he said.

Mom looked innocent. "Whatever gave you that idea? The terms of the lease state firmly that tenants may not keep pets."

"The terms of the lease also state firmly that no fires are to be built in the courtyard," said Mr. Meaner, "yet that is precisely what your son did today."

"I did not!" put in Marcus.

"You did so!" said Zack. "You were cooking sausages."

"It wasn't a real fire," said Marcus. "It was only a flame."

"A portable barbecue perhaps?" suggested Mr. Meaner.

"Sort of," said Marcus.

"Now that's been sorted out," said Mom brightly, "perhaps you would..."

"Not so fast, Mrs. Whippersnapper," said Mr. Meaner. "Not so fast. There remains the matter of the pet lizard."

"He keeps it in his pocket," said Zack. Now the news was out, he was determined to make Marcus squirm.

"Indeed," said Mr. Meaner. "Turn out your pockets, young man."

"Just a minute!" said Mom. "You have no right to barge in here making demands like this!"

"I have every right, if I suspect you have broken the terms of your lease!" said Mr. Meaner.

Marcus turned out his pockets. A handkerchief. A matchbox car. Two old batteries. Six peanut shells. "And that's all," he said.

"It is not!" Zack made a lunge at Marcus, then, remembering what had happened last time he got his hands on Timothy, he changed his mind and stepped back, tripped over the coffee table, and stumbled back against the couch. The couch tipped over and Timothy was revealed, already halfway to cat size and hissing angrily as he grew.

"Sir," said Timothy politely to Mr. Meaner through the hiss, "I really must complain about the conduct of your son!"

Mr. Meaner stared at Timothy. His nose twitched frantically, and he sneezed six times. "Right!" he gasped, mopping his watering eyes. "That's it! I'm a patient man, but I've had enough. Consider yourself evicted. And may I say you have been most unsatisfactory tenants! Most!"

"And you've been a most unsatisfactory landlord!" said Mom. "Look at that doorstep! If I've tripped over it once, I've tripped over it a dozen times a day!"

"Then you should lift up your feet," said Mr. Meaner. "You have fourteen days to be out. Good day, Mrs. Whippersnapper!"

And that was that.

CHAPTER SIX

In Which the Whippersnappers Meet Petronella Patella

When the Meaners had gone, Mom put her face in her hands.

"Never mind, Mom," said Marcus. "Now we can find a nicer place to live. Somewhere where they won't mind about Timothy."

"You don't understand," said Mom faintly. "We lose our deposit if we're evicted. It'll be very difficult to get another place to rent without the money for a deposit."

"Oh." Marcus wasn't too sure what a deposit was, so Mom explained.

"A deposit is money you pay a landlord when you first rent a flat or house. It's a sort of insurance that you'll look after the place. You mostly get it back when you move to another place. Unless..."

"Unless what?"

"Unless you've done some damage and not fixed it up, or you've been legally evicted for nonpayment of rent or breaking the rules. That's the way it works in Blankstone Buildings, anyway."

"I see," said Marcus. "So it's my fault for keeping Timothy."

"It's my fault for *letting* you keep Timothy," said Mom. Then she smiled briefly. "But I'm not sorry I did. Timothy's life is more important than Mr. Meaner's rules."

"So what do we do now?" asked Marcus.

"I don't know." Mom turned to Timothy. "Timothy Whuffenpuffen, I don't suppose that, along with your other talents, you can grant wishes?"

Timothy bowed his head. "To my sorrow, Madam, I cannot. Is it your requirement, Master Marcus, that I blast your enemy Meaner with my flame?"

"No, don't!" said Mom quickly. "It's a beautiful idea, but heaven knows we're in enough trouble without that. If only we had the deposit back, I'd be *glad* to be leaving this hole!"

"We'll have to get it somewhere else, that's all," said Marcus. "Why don't we sell the picture of Great Uncle Hinkley to that woman who wanted it? After all, this is an emergency."

"I would," said Mom, "if only I'd thought to take her name."

"We'll have to advertise in the paper on Saturday," said Marcus, so they did.

NOTICE

**IF THE PERSON WHO
RECENTLY EXPRESSED INTEREST
IN PURCHASING THE PAINTING
"HINKLEY" BY EUPHEMIA HAYCOCK
WILL CONTACT THE OWNER,
SHE WILL HEAR SOMETHING
TO HER ADVANTAGE.**

"That should do it," said Mom. "Now we only have to hope she sees it."

A lot of people saw the advertisement, and a lot of people would have liked to have bought a painting by Euphemia Haycock; but Mom had not put in an address, so they didn't all arrive in a rush at Blankstone Buildings. Then, on Monday evening, there was a knock on the door. Timothy whooshed down to matchbox size and crawled into Marcus's pocket for safekeeping.

"Who is it?" called Mom.

"Petronella Patella," said a brisk voice. "I'm here about the painting."

"Of *course*!" whispered Mom. "*That* was the name. However could I have forgotten it?" She opened the door. "Good evening, Ms. Patella. I'm so glad you saw the advertisement."

"So am *I*," said Petronella Patella.

"Come in, and mind the step," said Mom, but she was too late. The woman had already stumbled over the uneven doorstep. "Oh, I am so sorry," began Mom, reaching out to catch her, but Petronella Patella wasn't there to be caught. She had somehow turned the stumble into a double back flip across the room.

"My goodness!" said Mom. "I'm so sorry about the step."

Petronella Patella bounced back to her feet and dusted off her hands. She was a small woman with dark hair pulled back in a smooth bun, and bright eyes. "No harm done," she said shortly. "When you've been in the business as long as I have, it gets to be second nature."

"What business?" asked Marcus.

Petronella's gaze swiveled around to Marcus, and her eyes seemed to flash. "The circus business, of course, boy! Could I have forgotten to tell you last time I came?"

"Marcus wasn't here," said Mom. "And we only discussed the painting."

"So we did," said Ms. Patella. "A charming likeness of the subject, is it not?"

"Did you know Great Uncle Hinkley, then?" asked Marcus.

"Naturally, I do. I was chief clown in his Circus of Wonder for te... I mean two years! I worked with the Flying Gonzaloonies."

"Really!" said Mom faintly.

"Really. We were to be married, you know, Hinkley and I." Ms. Patella whisked out a small diamond-patterned handkerchief and dabbed her eyes with it.

"I see," said Mom. "Well, we still have the painting, as you can see."

"Oh yes." Petronella Patella glanced at the painting again. "Yes. Can you take a check?"

Mom gulped. "Oh – er, yes, of course."

Ms. Patella pulled out a checkbook. She signed a check and handed it to Mom, then sat down. "I wonder if I might have a cup of tea?"

"Of course," said Mom. "Marcus, you talk to Ms. Patella while I put the kettle on."

Petronella patted the lumpy couch next to her. "Sit down, Marcus, and tell me about yourself. You're very like Hinkley, aren't you?"

Marcus blushed. He began to tell Ms. Patella about himself, but he had the feeling she wasn't really listening, and wasn't really surprised when she interrupted.

"Tell me," said Petronella, "how is Timothy?"

"T-Timothy?" stammered Marcus.

"Yes, Timothy Whuffenpuffen. I trust he arrived here safely? I should hate to think he had been lost in transit."

"Oh," said Marcus.

"Is he here now?" asked Petronella. "I really should like to talk to him concerning Hinkley.

You *see*..." She dropped her voice and leaned so close that Marcus felt her warm breath on his ear. "I have reason to believe Hinkley has disappeared."

CHAPTER SEVEN

In Which
Marcus Whippersnapper
Flies Away

Marcus felt his head begin to spin.

Mom believed Great Uncle Hinkley was dead. Timothy Whuffenpuffen believed Great Uncle Hinkley had gone to a better place.

Now here was Petronella Patella with yet another theory – that Great Uncle Hinkley had simply disappeared, if a disappearance *could* be simple. It was all too much for him to follow, and he didn't know what to think. "I understand," he said weakly.

"I doubt it," said Petronella briskly. "And whether you do or you don't hardly matters. What *does* matter is that I must speak with Timothy, who will be of great assistance in my search for Hinkley. Did you say Timothy was here?"

"No," said Marcus.

Petronella frowned. "But I trust he *did* arrive?"

"Hmmm," said Marcus. "I don't know if I should talk to you about Timothy."

"Come on," said Petronella persuasively. "Either you have him or you don't. As to whether you should talk about him – really, what harm can talk do? Timothy is well able to look after himself."

"Yes, yes, he is," said Marcus, glad to be able to answer something with certainty.

"Well, where is he?" asked Petronella.

"Actually, he's in my pocket right now. Timothy?" He opened his pocket and Timothy clambered out and obligingly grew to small-cat size.

"Well, Timothy!" said Petronella Patella. "We meet again."

"Madam Pet," said Timothy, "you are looking very well."

Marcus watched them, mildly jealous. Timothy Whuffenpuffen was *his* dragon, not Petronella's.

"Timothy," said Petronella Patella, "I need your help."

"If it pleases Master Marcus, Madam Pet," said Timothy, and his jewel-blue eyes swiveled around toward Marcus.

Petronella Patella gave a dry bark of laughter. "Still the same old courteous Timothy! Marcus won't mind, will you, Marcus?"

"What sort of help do you want?" asked Marcus.

"It's like this...," said Petronella Patella; but before she could say more, Mom had come back with the tea cups, and Amanda Barton-Boote, as usual, had clattered in without knocking. She stared at Petronella Patella – and at Timothy.

"Marcus, what are you doing? Why are you letting *her* see Timothy? Her hair looks like it's painted on."

Petronella gave another short, sarcastic laugh. "Another loyal friend and defender of Timothy Whuffenpuffen, I presume. How lucky he is to have so many who care for his welfare!"

Amanda looked doubtful. "Who are you? What are you doing here? And how do you know about Timothy?" she asked.

Petronella frowned at Amanda. "My word, what a lot of questions!" she said. "Have you never been told that little children shouldn't talk too much?"

"This is Ms. Patella, Amanda," broke in Mom. "She is an old friend of Marcus's Great Uncle Hinkley, and of Timothy. She's here to buy our painting."

"That's true," said Petronella happily. "There is, however, just one tiny matter more."

"That's right," said Marcus. "You want Timothy to help you."

"I do indeed. You see, I have decided to mount an expedition to find Hinkley," said Petronella, "and a flying dragon represents a good saving on airfares."

Marcus and Amanda gaped at Timothy. Somehow, it had never occurred to them that he might be able to carry them through the air. But, when you come to think of it – why not? He was a flying dragon who could be any size he wished. Once he must have carried his first Master Whippersnapper on his escape from Dragonreign.

"Well?" said Petronella. "May I borrow Timothy?"

"I – I suppose so," said Marcus.

"But we want a receipt," said Amanda sharply.

"Very businesslike, aren't you?" said Petronella, giving Amanda a hard look.

"I need to be," said Amanda, staring right back.

"Timothy?" said Marcus.

Timothy coughed. "I have no objections, Master Marcus. Providing, of course, that you come as well."

Of course, Mom was not happy about the idea of Marcus flying off with Petronella Patella and Timothy. On the other hand, she had to find somewhere else to live – and soon. Without the money Petronella was paying for the painting, there would be no deposit for the new flat. And somehow, Mom had a feeling that the sale of the painting hinged on borrowing Timothy. True, Petronella *had* signed the check, but Mom knew perfectly well that checks could be torn up, or stopped at the bank.

"Well – all right, then" she said reluctantly. "But you must take great care of Marcus, and bring him back within a week. We have to find a new place to live."

Petronella was looking rather put out. "I don't need to take Marcus with me, Mrs. Whippersnapper. Surely you can trust Timothy to me."

But Timothy was shaking his head. "I regret, Madam Pet, that I cannot leave this place without Master Marcus. My contract forbids my residence with any but a flame-haired scion of the Whippersnappers."

"But we are going to find Hinkley," pointed out Petronella.

"We hope to find Master Hinkley," said Timothy. "We have no assurance that we shall succeed."

"All right," said Petronella, "Marcus may come. We'll leave at once."

She handed the check to Mom, and turned away.

"What about the painting?" asked Mom.

"The painting? Oh, yes. Might as well take it with me." Petronella Patella unhooked the painting from the wall. "I shall drop this off at my home on the way," she said.

Because they were being evicted, Mom had already begun to pack Marcus's clothes, so

now she handed him a bulging bag and a toothbrush. "Will he need a passport?" she asked nervously.

"Of course not," said Petronella happily. "One of the great advantages of traveling on dragon-back, my dear Mrs. Whippersnapper, is that you can avoid all that legal red tape. Now, Timothy, if you please!"

It was nearly dark when they went down to the courtyard. Amanda kept a sharp

lookout for Mr. Meaner and Zack, while Timothy took a deep breath and inflated himself to the height of a medium-sized elephant, then crouched so that Petronella and Marcus could climb aboard.

But I don't want to do this! thought Marcus, horrified. I don't want to do this at all!

Mom suddenly shook herself. "I'm sorry, but I can't possibly allow Marcus to go," she said. "I don't know what I was thinking of."

"Perhaps you were thinking of dear Hinkley," said Petronella, in a steely voice. "Alone – lost – perhaps captured by brigands. Perhaps being starved and beaten by uncivilized persons..."

"But what will you do if you find him?" persisted Mom. "And what if he *has* been kidnapped?"

"Then I'll call the police," said Petronella. "Surely you didn't think I'd be foolish enough to take on the kidnappers myself?"

"Can't Amanda come, too?" asked Marcus.

"Yes!" said Amanda gleefully.

"No!" said Petronella Patella. "I would have to have permission from her parents, and perhaps in the circumstances that might be difficult. You see, they don't know me."

"Mrs. Whippersnapper doesn't know you either!" said Amanda jealously, but Petronella just smiled.

"Ah, but Timothy does, and I do happen to be engaged to marry Hinkley (if we can find him). That makes me part of the family!"

She vaulted up onto Timothy's back, just behind the wings. "Climb aboard, Marcus, and hold on tight!" she cried.

Somehow, Marcus found himself sitting on Timothy's back, clutching Petronella Patella around the waist.

"Marcus, telephone me every day!" yelled Mom anxiously.

HELP! screamed Marcus to himself, but it was too late. Timothy gave a great sweep with his wings, and sprang into the air.

CHAPTER EIGHT

In Which Petronella Patella Changes Her Tune

As Timothy rose above Blankstone Buildings, Marcus opened his mouth in another silent scream. Then there was a swoop and a dive, and his stomach seemed to rise up until he almost choked. After that, he closed his eyes and concentrated on not fainting with terror. This is Timothy, he thought desperately. This is Timothy. Timothy would never hurt me. Timothy is contracted in blood to guard the flame-haired scion of the Whippersnappers...

It was cold, and after awhile, he opened his eyes a crack. "W-where are we?" he quavered.

"Flying," said Petronella Patella unhelpfully. "To my place, and then on to the last known address of *dear* Hinkley." There was an odd note in her voice. Almost, thought Marcus, as if she didn't *like* Great Uncle Hinkley. And that was very odd, since she intended to marry him.

"Ch-Chigwell Drive. In Meadow-upon-Woad! Wherever that is."

"Correct," said Petronella Patella. "Faster, Timothy."

"What?" Marcus thought he couldn't have heard correctly, and he felt Timothy falter slightly.

"*Faster*, Timothy," repeated Petronella. "I want to go top speed."

"Well, I don't!" snapped Marcus.

"Madam Pet, I must obey Master Marcus," said Timothy.

"Oh, all right," said Petronella and, after another few minutes, "Go down here." Marcus opened his eyes and saw that Timothy was spiraling down slowly over a dark house on the edge of town. But what town? He had no idea. When they landed, Petronella dismounted and hurried into the dark house. "Wait here," she said over her shoulder.

"What's wrong with her?" asked Marcus, still perched on Timothy's back. "She seems awfully cross. Wouldn't you think she'd be *glad* you agreed to help?"

"I do not know, Master Marcus," said Timothy. "She certainly seems less talkative than I had remembered."

"What do you mean remembered?" asked Marcus suspiciously. "Wasn't she around with you and Great Uncle Hinkley just recently?"

Timothy Whuffenpuffen shrugged. "Oh no, Master Marcus. Petronella Patella left the Circus of Wonder some time ago. It was a sad loss in some ways, for she was the only person who could control the Flying Gonzaloonies. But no doubt Master Hinkley had his reasons for dismissing her."

"But why didn't you say so before?" asked Marcus. "*She* made it sound quite different."

"It would have been most discourteous to interrupt a lady, and besides, no one asked me," said Timothy.

"I see," said Marcus. He knew just what Amanda Barton-Boote would have said to that, but, of course, it was Timothy all over. "She's not being very courteous to us, though, is she?" he ventured. "I suppose... I suppose we *could* just fly home again," he added, but by then it was too late. Petronella Patella was running back, carrying two blankets. She gave one to

Marcus and wrapped one around herself. "Hurry!" she told Timothy. "I want to get out of here before – oh, *bother* it. Too late!" A car was roaring up the driveway, with its headlights on high beam. The motor was still running when a figure leaped out.

"Petronella Patella! Stop right where you are! Stop!"

"Timothy, fly north," snapped Petronella. "Full speed."

"Madam Pet, would it not be courteous to see what this person...?"

"I know what he wants," snapped Petronella. "And he jolly well can't have it. Go, go, *go*!"

Timothy sprang into the air, and Marcus nearly swallowed his stomach again as the headlights dazzled him, and a horn and a yell blared out. "Rent! Rent!"

"Wh-what was that about?" he gulped, as soon as he could speak. By then, they were flying so fast he had to duck his face in under the blanket to be able to talk.

"A blasted journalist," said Petronella, after a moment's thought. "He's always after me. Always wanting mon–, I mean, always wanting interviews." She sighed. "It's dreadful to be both rich and famous, Marcus. You never get any privacy."

"Oh," said Marcus. He had heard that some journalists did make a nuisance of themselves chasing actors and singers around with cameras, but why was this one yelling about rent?

And, surely, if Petronella Patella were all *that* famous, wouldn't he have heard of her before?

And, surely, if she were all *that* rich, wouldn't she have bought an airplane ticket like anyone else?

"T-Timothy," he said, "would you please fly a bit slower? The wind's getting in my mouth."

"Close your mouth, then," said Petronella.

"Timothy?"

"Listen, boy," said Petronella, "have you ever heard the saying about too many cooks?"

"Yes, they spoil the broth," said Marcus.

"Well, too many drivers spoil the dragon," she said. "I'm in charge of this expedition, so you just pipe down. Clear?"

"OK," muttered Marcus. Petronella Patella had really changed her tune, and he made up his mind that as soon as they landed and Petronella got off, he was going to tell Timothy to fly him home.

Unfortunately, when they *did* eventually land later that night, he was much too tired to do anything except roll onto a heap of something soft and prickly and fall deeply asleep.

When Marcus woke early the next morning, he blinked around in bewilderment. He was lying in a pile of hay which was white with frost. *Frost*! Why was he lying in frost? Or – "Timothy? TIMothy!" he cried.

"Good morning, Master Marcus!" came Timothy's precise voice, and Timothy's tiny head poked out of Marcus's shirt pocket.

"Where are we?" asked Marcus, sitting up.

Timothy's jeweled eyes blinked thoughtfully. "We are in a Scottish meadow, Master Marcus. A short distance from the village of Meadow-upon-Woad, onetime address of the Circus of Wonder. If you care to cast your eyes to the left, you may be able to see the remains of a tree

uprooted (quite inadvertently) by one of our elephants, six months ago."

"Oh," said Marcus. Now he remembered why he was where he was. "But how could we have gotten here in just a couple of hours?" he asked. "It's hundreds of miles to Scotland."

Timothy looked modest. "I was instructed to fly at top speed, Master Marcus, and top speed to a dragon is no mean velocity."

"Oh," said Marcus again. "Where's that Petronella?"

"Madam Pet has gone to investigate the whereabouts of Master Hinkley," said

Timothy. "She was most displeased to find the Circus of Wonder departed from this place."

"But she said Great Uncle Hinkley had disappeared!" objected Marcus. "So she must have known he wouldn't be here."

"Quite so," said Timothy. "Her behavior is most strange. But now, if I may suggest it, shall we have some breakfast?"

Marcus was in favor of that, anyway, so Timothy toasted some bread.

"We could go home now, couldn't we?" suggested Marcus, shivering. "It's pretty cold out here."

"I have given my word to Madam Pet that I shall remain here," said Timothy.

"Oh," said Marcus. It occurred to him that he had been saying "oh" rather a lot, so he said "I see," as well. "Do you have to keep your word to her?" he asked. "I mean, she sort of hijacked us, didn't she?"

"True," said Timothy, "but I am sure Master Hinkley will help us. If we can find him."

"Oh." But Marcus couldn't help thinking Great Uncle Hinkley had already caused him quite enough trouble as it was.

CHAPTER NINE

In Which the Adventurers Visit Niwanabwanaland and Petronella Patella Explains

Petronella came back scowling. "He's done a runner," she growled.

"Who's done a runner?" asked Marcus. "Great Uncle Hinkley?"

"Who else? Now let's be off."

"Off where?"

"Full of questions, aren't you?" said Petronella sourly. "To Niwanabwanaland, I think."

Marcus thought he had a right to be full of questions. After all, he'd been carried off from Blankstone Buildings to a meadow outside Meadow-upon-Woad already, and now it seemed he was due to go somewhere called Niwanabwanaland. And where on Earth was that?

"Niwanabwanaland is in Africa, I apprehend?" said Timothy politely.

"Of course," said Petronella. "That's another of his favorite places." She sniffed. "He always seemed to favor spots that are out of the way. Anyone would think he had something to hide."

Or someone to hide *from*, thought Marcus. Could Great Uncle Hinkley be in trouble with the law?

"To Niwanabwanaland, Timothy," said Petronella Patella. "Full speed ahead."

"No!" said Marcus firmly. "*Home*, Timothy! Half speed ahead."

Timothy's eyes turned anxiously from one to the other, as he inflated to elephant size.

Marcus scrambled aboard. "*Go*, Timothy!" he yelled, and Timothy leaped from the ground.

Petronella Patella leaped also, high in the air, leapfrogging over Marcus's shoulders, to land lightly on Timothy's back.

"Niwanabwanaland, Timothy," said Petronella. It sounded as if she were talking through gritted teeth. "Go directly to Niwanabwanaland. Or else."

"Or else *what*?" asked Marcus rudely. "What

could you ever do to Timothy?"

"He has to sleep sometime," said Petronella grimly.

Marcus shivered. Petronella was horrible. How *could* Great Uncle Hinkley have wanted to marry her? "You'd better do as she says, Timothy," he said, "for now."

Back at Blankstone Buildings, Mom was getting worried. A week had passed since Marcus had flown away with Timothy Whuffenpuffen and Petronella Patella, and she had heard nothing from them at all.

"I told him to telephone every day," she said aloud. "I *told* him."

"Told him what?" asked Amanda Barton-Boote.

Mom jumped. "I didn't hear you come in, Amanda," she said.

"No. I crept. I didn't want old Meaner seeing me," said Amanda flatly.

"I don't blame you," said Mom. She gave a rather weak laugh. "Do you know, Amanda, sometimes I find myself wondering if I dreamed it all."

"Dreamed what?"

"About Marcus – Timothy Whuffenpuffen – that Patella woman. I mean, a patella is a *kneecap* for heaven's sake! I *didn't* dream it, did I? I really *do* have a son named Marcus who flew off with a clown named Patella on an expandable dragon in search of a missing Great Uncle, haven't I?"

"Of course you have," said Amanda.

Mom sighed. "That's a relief. I thought for awhile there I was really going crazy."

As far as Amanda could see, all adults were crazy, but she kindly didn't say so.

"I mean," said Mom, "it doesn't sound very likely, does it?"

Amanda shrugged. "Not very. But it did happen. Haven't you heard from them at all?"

"No," said Mom, "and that worries me. I was sure Marcus would telephone me every day."

"He is the telephoning sort," agreed Amanda. "Oh, I knew I should have gone to keep an eye on them."

Just then, the telephone did ring. Mom went to answer it and came back looking pale and frightened.

"Now what?" said Amanda. She wished Marcus and Timothy would come back. It was boring without anyone to boss around. "That was the bank manager," said Mom faintly. "Do you remember I sold the Euphemia Haycock painting of Great Uncle Hinkley to Petronella Patella?"

"Yes," said Amanda. "What about it?"

"She paid me by check," said Mom hollowly.

Amanda hooked her thumbs in her waistband. "Don't tell me, let me guess. The check just bounced?"

"How did you know?"

Amanda shrugged. "That's what checks do. Plus, I didn't like that Patella woman," she said. "That's why I wanted to go with Marcus. So now you haven't got the money for a deposit on your next flat, and she's got the painting."

"Yes," said Mom. "And even worse – she's got Marcus!"

Mom called the police, of course, but the story she told them didn't sound very convincing, even to her.

"All right, Mrs. –" (The sergeant looked down at his notebook.) "Mrs. Whippersnapper.

Let's take it once more from the top. Your son Mark–"

"Marcus," said Mom.

"Your son Marcus Whippersnapper has gone on a vacation with his great uncle's fiancée. Is that correct?"

"Not exactly a vacation," said Mom.

"And the lady's name is Petroleum Kneecap, is that right?"

Mom breathed deeply. "Petronella Patella," she said clearly.

The sergeant nodded. "And you're worried because your son hasn't telephoned you as expected. Tell me, what make of car does this Ms. Patella drive?"

"Heavens, *I* don't know!" said Mom. "She wasn't driving it, anyway."

"A bus tour, perhaps?" suggested the sergeant.

"No!" snapped Mom. "They flew."

"Ah." The sergeant became more businesslike. "Perhaps you could supply their flight reservation numbers..."

But Mom couldn't do that.

"Hmm. And I understand from your landlord that you have been given notice to vacate your apartment?"

"What's that got to do with it?" asked Mom.

"Perhaps you have not been in a very settled frame of mind, Mrs. Whippersnapper..."

"Perhaps I haven't," said Mom sharply. "But that check bounced and Marcus hasn't called and you can't get around that."

The sergeant couldn't; but other than suggest that Mom should report Petronella to the collection agency, he didn't have much advice to offer, and went away.

"I could see he thought I was quite crazy," said Mom angrily to Amanda. "But I suppose it does sound unlikely... Oh dear, what am I going to do?"

"I suppose," said Amanda, "we'll have to go and rescue him ourselves. Have you got anything you can pawn?"

***

Niwanabwanaland was more or less as Marcus would have expected – hot, steamy, and jungle-covered. Immense butterflies zoomed around, and giant flowers drooled hungrily from vines as thick as Marcus's thigh.

It was very hot, and Marcus found himself

sticking to Timothy's scales, just as you stick to a plastic-covered armchair in the summer. "Ugh!" he said, peeling one leg away from the scales and nearly overbalancing himself.

"Watch out!" said Petronella. "I don't want you falling off. Now, Timothy, I want you to fly in long sweeps back and forth over the jungle. And you, boy, keep your eyes peeled for signs."

"Signs of what?" asked Marcus.

Petronella sighed with exasperation. "Signs of the circus, of course!"

"Why would he be at the circus if he's disappeared?" asked Marcus.

Petronella sighed. "You're not a very *bright* child, Marcus, are you? Hinkley, of course, disappeared and took the circus with him."

"Then why are you worried about him?" asked Marcus.

"I'm not worried about the old brute," said Petronella. "I just want to find him and make him face up to his obligations."

"What obligations?"

"His obligations as a husband-to-be," said Petronella. "Marcus, your Uncle Hinkley is a devious man. I'd made him agree to marry me

– which took some doing, I can tell you – and then the brute dropped me off in Paris to buy my wedding dress."

"Yes? Then what?"

"Then nothing," said Petronella. "I haven't seen him since. He didn't answer my letters, and I didn't know where he was. I was stranded."

"But, Uncle Hinkley wouldn't do that," said Marcus.

"Oh, wouldn't he!" said Petronella sourly.

"It is true, Master Marcus," said Timothy. "While Madam Pet was shopping for the necessary garment, Master Hinkley made a snap decision to move the Circus of Wonder to Kathmandu. I did suggest it was an extremely discourteous thing to do, but Master Hinkley was quite determined to abandon her."

"Of course, I followed," said Petronella grimly, "but by the time I'd arrived there (by llama, if you please!), the sneaky wretch had moved on again."

"To Antarctica," said Timothy.

"And again!" said Petronella angrily. "And finally, I ran out of funds. Then I looked up my contact at Hinkley's solicitors – Mr. McDaftie. He told me Hinkley had been in touch with him regarding Timothy here. I also discovered that Timothy had been sent to you and your mother as Hinkley's only living relatives, Marcus. That's why I came to you."

Marcus sighed. He wished Petronella hadn't come to him, but she had, and now he was stuck with her. In Niwanabwanaland.

※ ❦ ※

For some days, Timothy zoomed back and forth from morning until dark. Niwanabwanaland was a huge place, and Petronella insisted on scanning every hill and wrinkle for signs of Great Uncle Hinkley or the Circus of Wonder. They spent the nights uncomfortably under giant trees, and as soon as the sun rose, Petronella had Timothy flying again. Back and forth, back and forth. Marcus had a headache from the heat, and he found himself wanting to push Petronella off Timothy's back. He might have tried it, too, but he knew it wouldn't work. Petronella was an acrobat, and she'd be bound to grab a handhold somehow and flip herself back into position. Besides, he didn't want to hurt her. He just wanted her to take him home.

Back and forth. Back and forth. "There's something," he said doubtfully at last. "It sort of looks like a bunch of tents..."

"Aha!" breathed Petronella. "The Circus of Wonder! I knew we'd find it eventually. Fly lower, Timothy... Ah, yes... I can see a man! It must be Hinkley..." Then she gave a startled exclamation and clapped a hand to her cheek. "The ungrateful brute is *shooting* at us! Hinkley – how *dare* you!"

CHAPTER TEN

In Which Marcus Meets Antony Andrew Winterbottom

Ping! Ping! Small, hard objects bounced off Timothy's scales, and Marcus ducked. With a small corner of his mind, he wondered why he wasn't screaming with terror. He ought to have been practically dead with fright, but somehow his main emotion was anger.

Anger with whoever was shooting at them from below.

Anger with Petronella Patella for involving him in her determined pursuit of Great Uncle Hinkley. (Fancy wanting to marry a man who obviously didn't want to marry her!)

Anger with Great Uncle Hinkley for vanishing in the first place.

Anger with Timothy Whuffenpuffen for being too polite to warn him about Petronella's ruthless side before they had ever left Blankstone Buildings.

Anger at himself for not insisting on staying at home.

That amounted to a lot of anger, and it built up and up until, like a huge surge of pressure in a steam engine, it had to find a release. "STOP THAT!" yelled Marcus suddenly. "STOP THAT AT *ONCE!*" The effort of yelling so loudly hurt his throat, so he had to cough before he went on, more quietly, and told Timothy to land.

"Are you quite sure, Master Marcus?" asked Timothy.

"Yes, I'm sure," said Marcus. "I'm sick of being whizzed all over the place, and if we get down behind some trees, he won't be able to aim his gun."

Timothy taxied down between the trees. "I don't think it's a gun, Master Marcus. Guns damage dragon hide, and I am quite undamaged. I think it's probably a peashooter."

"A peashooter!" gasped Marcus. He heard himself give a silly giggle. "You mean someone's shooting peas at us? Is that all it is? I thought it was bullets at least!"

Again, he wondered why he wasn't half-dead with fright.

Timothy did not answer, for by now they had landed just outside the clearing occupied by the Circus of Wonder.

"All right," said Marcus firmly to Petronella Patella. "Get off. Go and tell Great Uncle Hinkley – if it is him – to stop shooting peas at us. Then we'll leave you to it."

"No," said Petronella. "That won't do at all. What if Hinkley proves to be stubborn?"

"It will do very well," said Marcus. "You wanted to get to the Circus of Wonder, now you're here. It's up to you to deal with Uncle Hinkley, if we don't get shot first. Now go and find that peashooter."

Stunned by Marcus's determination, Petronella vaulted down from Timothy's back, but it was too late – the peashooter had found *them.* A perfect hail of peas began to fall around them.

"HINKLEY!" yelled Petronella. "Come out here and face up to your responsibilities like a *man!*"

The fellow with the peashooter advanced cautiously, weapon at the ready. As he came closer, Marcus could see that this weapon was a long piece of bamboo with a mouthpiece at one end.

"Hinkley!" said Petronella threateningly. "You put that weapon away at once! I've told you and told..." Her voice trailed off uncertainly. "You're not Hinkley!" she said.

"I never said I was," retorted the man, staring at Timothy. "And you're not the Flying Gonzaloonies. My word – what a splendid dragon! Are you donating it to my circus?"

"Your circus?" humphed Petronella. "It belongs to Hinkley Whippersnapper. My fiancé."

"Oh, I know," said the peashooter. "But it's mine in a manner of speaking; I've signed a contract to manage it for a seven-year term. And now I'm wishing I hadn't."

The fellow with the peashooter was a tall young man with pink, scrubbed-looking cheeks and an old-fashioned blazer.

"I mean to *say*," he said, as Petronella stared at him in outrage, "it's all very well to leave the old ancestral acres and join a circus – jolly exciting and all that, and my dad was furious – but I'm afraid I'm making rather a hash of running it. I'm actually much better at managing a motel, which is what I was doing before this offer came up.

"And now the weight lifters are on strike, the elephant's in a sulk, and the Flying Gonzaloonies won't fly. They've all gone off in a huff, and they keep on making guerrilla raids on the tents. I thought you were them, flying down to mutiny against me or something."

"Why seven years?" asked Marcus. "And what's your name?"

The young man shrugged. "So sorry, old chap – I should have introduced myself before. I'm Antony Andrew Winterbottom." He moved the peashooter to his left hand, and held out his right.

"As for the seven years – the jolly old Circus of Wonder is entailed, and it has to go to the old man's heir when the young Whippersnapper turns eighteen. Or so I'm told." He sighed. "I jolly well wish the lad luck. He'll need it if he has to deal with the Flying Gonzaloonies. Not to mention the elephant."

Then he looked admiringly at Petronella. "I say, you dismounted from that dragon in a jolly handy way, old girl – is it possible that you might know something about running a circus? If not, I'm afraid I'll have to stir up Old Man Whippersnapper out of Nowhere Else and hand it over – otherwise, there won't be any circus for the young Whippersnapper to inherit, and I don't want *that* on my conscience." And he looked gloomy.

Marcus stared. "You mean, Great Uncle Hinkley is alive? You know where he is?"

"Well, of course I do, old chap," said Winterbottom. "He's at Nowhere Else. I made it a condition of the contract that I had to know where he was. You see, between you and me, I hadn't the greatest confidence in my ability to run a circus, and I wanted to be able to hand it back to the owner if it got beyond me." He sighed lugubriously. "And I'm afraid I was right."

Petronella Patella was glaring at Marcus. "So it's you who's going to have the Circus of Wonder! A red-headed brat without a triple back flip to his name!"

Marcus glared back at her. "I've got something better than a triple back flip," he said. "I've got Timothy. And if you come one step closer, Petronella Patella, I'll leave you right here and fly home! Watch her, Timothy, and let me know if she makes a move." He turned his attention to Antony Andrew Winterbottom. "Mr. Winterbottom, my name is Marcus Whippersnapper, and this is Timothy Whuffenpuffen. The woman is Petronella Patella, and she says she's a clown. Now, all three of us want to find Great Uncle Hinkley, so could you tell us where he is? 'Nowhere Else' doesn't sound like a proper address to me."

"Well, it is," said Winterbottom cheerfully. "I checked it out. I'm not as green as I look, young Whippersnapper. And to prove it, I'll take you there. Er – can your dragon carry three?"

Mom began to wring her hands, then changed her mind and dusted them off instead. "Amanda, I know what I'm going to do! I'm going to see Mr. McDaftie. I think it's time he explained a few things."

"Great!" said Amanda. "I'm coming, too!"

Mom did take Amanda with her to McDaftie, McDaftie, and McDaftie. "Otherwise," she said, "I'll start wondering again if I'm imagining things. With you along, I'll have someone to back me up."

"With Mr. McDaftie?" asked Amanda. She liked the idea of herself as a backer-upper.

"No," said Mom grimly, "with myself." She

put on her jacket and combed her hair. "Just in case I start doubting my sanity again."

As they were leaving, Zack Meaner made a face at them over the railings. "Found a place to live yet, Mrs. Whippersnapper?" asked Zack.

"No, if it's any business of yours," said Mom.

"Well, I happen to know my auntie's got a nice dog kennel for rent," said Zack. "She might be willing to let you have it – at a price."

Mom tossed her head. "How I dislike that boy," she said. "But maybe he's not really to blame. I mean, look at his father!"

CHAPTER ELEVEN

In Which Mom and Amanda Bother Mr. Fergus McDaftie and Seven Visitors Arrive at Nowhere Else

Mr. Fergus McDaftie was a dried-up, elderly gentleman. He drank tea made from real tea leaves, which he strained through his mustache. He did *not* want to see Mrs. Veronica Whippersnapper.

"Oh dear," he said, when his secretary announced Mom. "Another of those Whippersnappers. They're bound to bother me. I always knew I should never have taken on that man Hinkley as a client."

"You couldn't avoid it," pointed out his secretary. "Your father acted for his father."

"More's the pity." Fergus McDaftie blotted some tea leaves from his mustache, and put his hand over his eyes. "Whippersnappers! Circuses! Dragons!" he whispered. "Oh no, no, it isn't *fair*! She'll *bother* me. Tell her I'm not here."

"Mr. McDaftie," said Mom, who had come in behind the secretary, "that is a lie. You are *so* here, and I *am* going to bother you. I am Veronica Whippersnapper, niece-in-law of your client, Mr. Hinkley Q. Whippersnapper."

Fergus McDaftie cleared his throat and polished his spectacles. "Er – yes, Mrs. Whippersnapper? Do you have a problem?"

"I'll say," said Mom.

"And is this little lady your daughter?" said Fergus McDaftie, playing for time. "Dear me, how very like you she is! The resemblance is remarkable."

"Well, it shouldn't be," said Amanda, staring at Fergus McDaftie. "My name's Amanda Barton-Boote, and I look just like my Grandfather Barton-Boote. So there."

After that, Fergus McDaftie was more embarrassed than ever, but Mom wasn't in the mood to be given the runaround.

"Look here, Mr. McDaftie," she said, planting both hands on the desk and leaning across it, "we need some help."

"Er – of a *legal* nature?"

"Of a *practical* nature," corrected Mom. "You see, it's like this. You remember that legacy you forwarded to my son Marcus from Great Uncle Hinkley?"

"Er –"

"It was a packaged dragon," said Mom sternly. "And you can't pretend you've forgotten that. There's something very memorable about a packaged dragon. I'm sure the Post Office thought so, too."

"I hope the creature hasn't been causing any problems. I did suggest to Hinkley..."

"The dragon isn't the problem," said Mom. "The problem is Petronella Patella." Fergus McDaftie had cowered back at the sound. "Ah, I see you are familiar with the name?"

"Er – yes, yes, I seem to have heard it somewhere," he said faintly.

"You told her where to find us in the first place," said Mom sternly.

"Well, in a manner of speaking –"

"Did you or didn't you?" put in Amanda.

She felt it was time she did some backing up.

"Yes," said Fergus McDaftie, even more faintly. "That is, I told her your names. I did not tell her your precise address."

"Sometimes a name is enough," said Mom, "when the name happens to be an unusual one like Whippersnapper. Once she knew we existed, she had only to check the phone books until she found us."

Fergus McDaftie looked hunted.

"The thing is, she did find us," said Mom. "She gained entry to our flat under false pretenses, pretending she had enough money to buy a painting. I'm sure she could just as readily pretended she wanted to sell us a vacuum cleaner if she'd happened to have had one in her pocket. I expect she was looking for Timothy then, but we hadn't received him."

"I see," said Mr. McDaftie, even more faintly.

"I didn't want to sell the painting then, but later it became necessary, and I played into her hands by advertising it in the paper," continued Mom. "She came, and I sold her a picture of Hinkley Whippersnapper, and the check bounced. She then asked for a cup of tea and used the interval while I boiled the water to weasel information out of my son, Marcus."

"Madam, we can hardly be held responsible..."

Mom brushed this aside. "Mr. McDaftie, I don't hold you responsible. I am merely trying to get at the truth. Petronella Patella arrived on our doorstep with two pieces of news. One was that she was engaged to be married to my son's great uncle. True or false?"

"True – er, false," said Fergus McDaftie. "I mean, true after a fashion, Mrs. Whippersnapper. However, the wedding did not take place, and I think we may reasonably consider the engagement terminated."

"The other piece of news was that Hinkley Whippersnapper may still be alive. True or false?"

Mr. McDaftie looked sheepish. "Madam, you must understand that my first obligation is to my client..."

"Mr. McDaftie, my son's safety may be at stake. Is Hinkley Whippersnapper alive?"

"Er – yes," said Fergus McDaftie. "At least, he was last time I had cause to communicate with him."

"Which was when and where?"

"Er – last Wednesday. In Nowhere Else."

"Aha!" said Mom. "Now we're getting somewhere! I take it he had not mysteriously vanished as of that date?"

"Mrs. Whippersnapper, whatever gave you that idea?" asked Fergus McDaftie.

"Petronella Patella," said Mom grimly. "Didn't she, Amanda? She led us to understand Hinkley Whippersnapper had disappeared under suspicious circumstances."

Amanda nodded. "And she took Timothy and Marcus off to find him, and they haven't come back."

"Nor telephoned us," said Mom. "So do you or do you not agree that it is imperative that you give us Hinkley Whippersnapper's exact, current address?"

Fergus McDaftie gulped. Then he drew a legal-looking pad toward him, uncapped a legal-looking pen, and began to write.

In the southwest of England, there is a place called Nowhere Else. It's a nice little place, with green grass and trees and mountains nearby. Deer live in the forests, and people walk their dogs along the grassy verges. Cows graze and children play. Yes, Nowhere Else is a very nice place. That's why Great Uncle Hinkley Whippersnapper chose it as a place to retire and write his autobiography. Of course, he had other reasons as well – both for the retirement and the choice of place.

His reasons for retirement were many and complicated, but sprang mostly from a dislike of being forced to talk before breakfast. Hinkley hated conversation before breakfast, and the Flying Gonzaloonies, an exceedingly talkative family of trapeze artists, insisted on it.

His choice of Nowhere Else as a place of retirement came about because he had a house there. It had been built by his maternal grandfather, Thomas Smith, at the turn of the century. Thomas Smith had not, of course, been a Whippersnapper, but his house, Calendar House, had a definite air of Whippersnapperishness about it, anyway.

It was a very big, very rambling house, and it had a window for every day of the year, a door for every day of the month, and a

staircase for every day of the week. Hinkley's grandfather had lived to be very old, and after he died, the house stood empty. And now, of course, Hinkley had hired a callow young manager named Antony Andrew Winterbottom for the Circus of Wonder, and moved into Calendar House.

No one connected him with the Circus of Wonder. Even if they had, they wouldn't have asked him about it. People in Nowhere Else are good at minding their own business.

Only two people in the whole world knew where he was: his solicitor and Antony

Andrew Winterbottom, who had proved to be shrewder than he looked, and who had insisted on having the information. But since Antony Andrew Winterbottom *and* the Circus of Wonder were camped in Niwanabwanaland without transportation, Hinkley felt confident there would be no interruptions from *that* quarter.

Great Uncle Hinkley enjoyed living in his grandfather's old house. There were so many rooms that he didn't have to bother with housework. As one room became dirty, he simply moved into another. He never had any visitors, but if any *had* arrived, he would have pretended not to be at home, especially before breakfast.

Then one day, seven visitors arrived all at once.

"Curses!" said Great Uncle Hinkley Whippersnapper, clasping his brow with a trembling hand. "Foiled again!"

CHAPTER TWELVE

In Which Great Uncle Hinkley Defends His Actions, but No One Is Impressed

The seven visitors arrived in two separate groups, and from two separate directions.

The first group consisted of Timothy Whuffenpuffen, Marcus Whippersnapper, Petronella Patella, and Antony Andrew Winterbottom.

The second group consisted of Mrs. Veronica Whippersnapper, Amanda Barton-Boote, and Fergus McDaftie.

"Hinkley, you rat!"

"Master Hinkley – you are safe!"

"Great Uncle Hinkley, I've been hijacked!"

"Mr. Whippersnapper, sir!" exclaimed one group.

"Marcus! Why didn't you call?"

"Mr. Whippersnapper, she made me do it!"

"Marcus! We've come to rescue you!" exclaimed the other group.

"Oh no!" exclaimed Great Uncle Hinkley Whippersnapper. He tore in through the front door, dashed through seventeen rooms, and ran out through the back, right into the arms of Petronella Patella, who had turned a handspring over the chimney to intercept him.

"I *thought* you'd try that, you rat!" said Petronella with satisfaction. "Face up to your responsibilities like a man!" And she gave him a good shake.

"Oh no!" said Great Uncle Hinkley again. "You found me. You all found me! What a waste of a mysterious disappearance." But no one was listening to him. Petronella Patella was shaking Great Uncle Hinkley. Mom was shaking Petronella Patella. Antony Winterbottom was gazing admiringly at Petronella. Timothy was growing and shrinking distractedly. Fergus McDaftie was gibbering and stammering excuses. And Amanda was jumping up and down, yelling at the top of her voice, "Marcus, Marcus! We've come to rescue you! Marcus! Do you hear me, Marcus? You're safe now!"

Marcus folded his arms and took a deep breath. "BE QUIET!" he bawled. "All of you!" Then he turned to Amanda. "Thanks, Amanda, but I don't need rescuing. I can manage quite well with Timothy."

Great Uncle Hinkley ducked under Petronella's arm and sprang over to shake Marcus by the hand. "Spoken like a true

Whippersnapper, great nephew! So glad to see you have everything under control. Now, if you'll just excuse me, I'll be off..."

"Oh, no you don't!" said Marcus. "There's been enough slipping off. You've got some explaining to do, Great Uncle Hinkley. Why did you pretend to be dead and vanished and gone to a better place?"

Great Uncle Hinkley's cheeks turned very red and so did his nose. "My boy," he said solemnly, "have you ever been in a situation where everybody persists in talking to you before breakfast, and you just want to duck out?"

"Often," said Marcus. "Especially when it's Amanda."

Great Uncle Hinkley exhaled a knowing sigh. "Then you understand my position."

"No," said Marcus, "I don't. I mean, you can't just drop everything and run like that. Not when there are people involved. And dragons. Not when you're a grown-up. You might have saved yourself some trouble, but you caused an awful lot for other people. And for Timothy."

"Unavoidable side effect," muttered Great Uncle Hinkley, but he shuffled his feet like a guilty boy.

Marcus took a deep breath. "What about Timothy?" he asked.

"What *about* Timothy? I sent him to you, the flame-haired scion of the Whippersnappers, as was entirely right and proper."

"But why didn't you ask us first? I mean, what if I hadn't been able to keep him?"

"Oh come on," said Great Uncle Hinkley. "You're a Whippersnapper, aren't you? I knew you'd look after him."

Timothy shuffled his wings. "He did, Master Hinkley," he said reproachfully, "and in doing so, he and Madam Whippersnapper have lost their home. Madam Pet has been put to great inconvenience and driven to dubious measures – including threats against my life – and Mr. Winterbottom has been forced to defend his person against the Flying Gonzaloonies with a peashooter."

"Yes, Marcus and I have lost our flat," put in Mom, "and Mr. McDaftie has been driven to breaking a confidence. And I've been worried *sick*. Uncle Hinkley, I think you owe us all an explanation. *And* an apology."

Great Uncle Hinkley drew himself up. "Oh, do you!" he said. "Well, while we're getting everything out on the table, you'd better listen yourselves." He turned to Mom. "I fail to see how you can hold me responsible for the loss of your apartment."

"That's easy," said Mom. "You wished Timothy on us (no offense, Timothy). Our landlord found out we were keeping a pet and evicted us."

"*And* kept their deposit money!" put in Amanda. "Mean old Meaner."

"Oh," said Uncle Hinkley. Then he perked up. "Granted, I may have been a little at fault in this matter, but how can I possibly be blamed for *your* indiscretion, Fergus? I trusted you to keep your mouth shut."

Fergus McDaftie shuddered. "They *looked* at me," he said. "Both of them. Mrs. Whippersnapper and the Barton-Boote brat... er, I mean, child. They looked at me, and I couldn't refuse to tell them where you were."

Great Uncle Hinkley looked uncomfortable. "But you, Petronella," he said stoutly, "you had no reason to make life a misery for me."

Petronella Patella glowered at him. "You deserted me," she said. "You left me in Paris with a wedding dress. If you'd only said you didn't want to get married, it would have been different. But there's something very humiliating about being left in Paris with a wedding dress. It sours a person."

"And as for *you*," said Great Uncle Hinkley, ignoring Petronella, and glaring at Antony Winterbottom, "how can you possibly blame me for *your* inadequacies? I warned you about the Flying Gonzaloonies. I warned you they were incessant talkers-before-breakfast."

"Oh, I say, old man," said Winterbottom. "Talking before breakfast I can stand – I mean, talking's normal. But those lads were a mutiny waiting to happen. You didn't tell me the weight lifters demanded crocodile steaks for every meal, either! You didn't tell me the elephant was emotionally attached to the biggest Flying Gonzaloonie, and would go into a violent decline when deprived of his company. There's a whole lot you didn't tell me about running a circus."

Great Uncle Hinkley looked abashed. "Well, you *would* try talking business before breakfast," he muttered. "And I still think you brought it all on yourselves. *ALL* of you." And he folded his arms.

Marcus took a deep breath. "Timothy didn't," he said. "None of this was Timothy's fault."

"Oh, *wasn't* it?" said Great Uncle Hinkley bitterly.

"Master Hinkley!" cried Timothy, "I trust you will not deem it impolite if I may be so bold as to ask in which way I offended?"

"That's the way you offended!" howled Great Uncle Hinkley. "You offended by being so enduringly, everlastingly EXEMPLARY, and so permanently, perpetually POLITE! Before breakfast! After lunch! During dinner! Prior to supper!

"'Master Hinkley this,' and 'Master Hinkley that' and 'Master Hinkley, please consider!' It was driving me mad. If I'd wanted a wife to mind my manners and morals, I'd have married one!"

"Oh," said Timothy, in a very small voice. "In that case, Master Hinkley, I gather we must consider our contract broken."

"Yes, yes, anything you like," said Great Uncle Hinkley. "Just *don't* be polite about it. I've put up with politeness for twenty-five years, and surely that's enough."

Timothy bowed his crested head.

"Oh, stop it," said Marcus. "Don't you know a broken contract means a dead dragon?" He patted the drooping Timothy. "Never mind, Timothy, you can be as polite to me as you like. And I'll keep you forever and ever – that is, unless I have a son to pass you on to. And when I inherit the Circus of Wonder, you can help me run that as well."

Mom looked stunned. "Marcus," she said, "what's all this about you inheriting the Circus of Wonder?"

"Yes," said Petronella. "What?"

Great Uncle Hinkley began to back away, but Petronella and Mom, united for once, grabbed an arm each and held him where he was. Amanda, not to be outdone, grabbed his legs.

"Had I forgotten to mention that?" asked Great Uncle Hinkley, looking shifty.

"You led me to believe it would be mine when we were married," said Petronella.

"But we're not married," said Great Uncle Hinkley plaintively, "so there won't be any little Whippersnappers."

"You *said*..." complained Petronella.

"I know. I said a lot of things, but you drove me to it with your everlasting talking. Anyway, I've no need of little Whippersnappers. I've been grooming Marcus for years for his eventual takeover."

"Oh, *have* you!" said Mom. "May I ask how? You'd never even set eyes on Marcus until today."

"Why do you think I sent all those animals?" demanded Great Uncle Hinkley. He frowned over his shoulder at Mom. "I was trying to get you used to the idea gradually, so to speak. Get you acclimatized. You can't say I didn't give you any hints. The penguin, for instance. And the llama. Aren't they prime pets for a potential circus owner?"

"The penguin and the llama had to go to the zoo," said Mom angrily. "As you'd have known if you'd ever bothered to read the letters *we* sent *you*."

"Letters, schmetters!" said Great Uncle Hinkley. "Never read the things. And how was I to know you'd be stupid enough to take a flat with an unreasonable landlord?"

"If anyone's being unreasonable around here," said Mom grimly, "it's you. And now I think you owe us all a cup of tea."

CHAPTER THIRTEEN

In Which Various Problems Are Solved to the Satisfaction of All

Great Uncle Hinkley led the way into Calendar House. He didn't have much choice in the matter because Petronella Patella and Mom were still holding his arms. Amanda, however, had let go of his legs.

"*What* a mess!" said Mom, frowning around the kitchen.

"Isn't it!" Amanda was deeply impressed.

"What *you* need, Uncle Hinkley, is someone to look after you," said Mom severely. "Clearly, the management of this place is beyond you. Perhaps you should move to a retirement village."

Great Uncle Hinkley looked annoyed. "Rubbish," he said. "I have a very simple system. I simply move from one room to the next as they become dirty. Unfortunately, I can't do that with the kitchen, because this is the only kitchen in the house."

"Disgusting," said Mom. She turned to Petronella. "Ms. Patella, I don't like people who bounce checks and con their way into apartments and fly away with boys and dragons under false pretenses."

Petronella scowled. "I suppose you think I ought to be sorry."

"You should be," said Mom, "but whatever you've done, you don't deserve the misery of marriage to Uncle Hinkley. He needs a housekeeper, not a wife. One with thick skin."

"You're quite right!" said Great Uncle Hinkley. "And you're hired."

"What?" Mom stared.

"You're hired," said Great Uncle Hinkley. "I need a housekeeper, you need somewhere to live. So you're hired. That should solve both our problems. But you can't talk to me before breakfast."

"No," said Mom flatly. "I won't be your housekeeper."

"You won't be his housekeeper?" said Petronella Patella, Fergus McDaftie, and

Amanda in chorus. "Why not?"

"Because," said Mom, "I don't want to be anyone's housekeeper. Not even for a place to live. You see, I haven't *got* a thick skin, and I don't think I could put up with your rudeness. Before *or* after breakfast."

"*I* wouldn't mind being your housekeeper," said Antony Winterbottom. "I may not be thick-skinned, but I *am* thickheaded. Or so my father says."

"But you're running the Circus of Wonder," objected Great Uncle Hinkley. "You won't have time."

"Strange you should say that, old man, but I really can't hack it, don't y'know," said Winterbottom. "Got to face the fact – I'm just not cut out for running circuses. Not with those Flying Gonzaloonies. Not to speak of the weight lifters and the elephant. On the other hand, I know I could run this house. No bother at all."

"Done!" said Great Uncle Hinkley. "You're fired. You're hired. That's one problem solved. Fergus, dissolve the circus contract and draw up a new one for young Winterbottom to housekeep at Calendar House."

118

"This is most irregular," muttered Fergus McDaftie, but Antony Winterbottom had already tied on an apron and was searching the cupboards for a box of tea. "I hope you find a good replacement manager for the Circus of Wonder, old chap," he said, as he measured tea leaves into the pot.

"So do I," said Great Uncle Hinkley. "I really would like to be left in peace to finish my autobiography. Fergus, I suppose *you* wouldn't know anyone interested in running a circus for a few years?"

"No, I would not," said Fergus McDaftie, and he buried his mustache in his cup of tea.

"Mom," said Marcus, tugging her arm.

"Not now, Marcus," said Mom.

"Mom, what about us?"

"Oh, we'll manage somehow, I suppose, Marcus," said Mom. "We always have."

"I mean, what about *us* running the Circus of Wonder? We could live in a caravan then."

"Yes," said Great Uncle Hinkley, swinging around to stare at Mom. "What about you? I always intended young Marcus to take over eventually, so why not now? There's a school quite nearby if you want him educated."

"Preposterous!" exploded Mom. She put her arm around Marcus's shoulders. "Great Uncle Hinkley, I suppose you mean well, but honestly, if you knew the kind of boy Marcus is, you wouldn't suggest such a thing, even in jest."

"I can see the kind of boy Marcus is," said Great Uncle Hinkley. "A veritable Whippersnapper. Brave, decided, strong-minded, stubborn, pigheaded, loud-voiced..."

Amanda laughed. "You're nuts!" she said. "Marcus isn't like that at all."

"Marcus couldn't do it," said Mom. "He's a dear boy, but he really isn't the sort of stuff of which circus owners are made."

"I wouldn't be too sure about that," muttered Petronella Patella. "He certainly told me where to get off."

"Oh, go home, Petronella, do," said Great Uncle Hinkley.

"I would if I could, but I can't," said Petronella glumly. "My landlord's after me for the rent."

Marcus stared at her. "So you're *not* rich and famous, and that man *wasn't* a journalist..."

"No," said Petronella. "He was a lurking landlord. Satisfied?"

"Well," said Mom, collecting herself. "I'm

sorry about all this, but I think we should leave you all to sort yourselves out. Come, Marcus, Amanda. Good-bye, Hinkley. I can't say it's been nice knowing you, because it hasn't. And as for your nonsense about Marcus taking on the circus... I've never heard such a silly thing in all my life! In fact, I'm not even sure I believe in the circus. *I've* never seen it."

Great Uncle Hinkley drew himself up. "I assure *you*, Veronica..."

"But, *Mom!*"

"Er-hm," said someone politely, and everyone turned to stare at Timothy Whuffenpuffen. "If I might say something?" he asked.

"Sure, go ahead," said Great Uncle Hinkley. "Everyone else has been sticking their beaks in, why should you be any different?"

Timothy's blue eyes swiveled anxiously from side to side. "I must confess it came as a sad blow to me to discover that I have been annoying you all these years with my courtesy," he said to Great Uncle Hinkley. "However, I *am* the senior person here, and I think myself a reasonable judge of character. Despite being so sorely mistaken in *yours* all these years."

And he shot an unfriendly look at Uncle Hinkley.

"I think, judging from my short acquaintance with him, that Master Marcus could do it. Given appropriate support and advice, naturally."

"Timothy, you're way off beam," said Mom. "Marcus would be far too nervous..."

Timothy shook his head. "I suggest that you may well find your son somewhat changed by his recent experiences. Are you feeling nervous about anything, Master Marcus?"

"No," said Marcus. "Only that Mom will say no. Come on, Mom – can't we look after the circus? You know you like animals – you always hated sending those others to the zoo. And we do need a place to live. A place where we can keep Timothy."

"Animals are all very well," said Mom, staring at Marcus, "but what about the people? I must say I don't like what I've heard about these Flying Gonzaloonies. If Hinkley couldn't manage them and Mr. Winterbottom couldn't manage them, probably no one else could, either. Let alone you and me."

"Oh, I can manage the Flying Gonzaloonies," said Petronella Patella. "I always could. I'd be happy to help – if it means I get my job back."

"So please?" said Marcus. "Please can we take over the Circus of Wonder?"

"Oh, all right," said Mom. "I'll probably regret this all my life, but then I'd probably regret it even more if I said no. There's just one thing..."

"What?"

"Where is this circus?"

Antony Winterbottom turned around from the stove. "By Jove!" he said. "If I didn't forget! I left it in Niwanabwanaland."

CHAPTER FOURTEEN

In Which All Ends Are Tied Up, and Marcus Lives Happily Ever After

Of course, they sorted it all out eventually. Timothy Whuffenpuffen expanded to the size of a giant dirigible, and he, Petronella, and Marcus flew back to Niwanabwanaland and fetched the Circus of Wonder. They did it in the middle of the night, but even so, there *were* a few rumors of giant dirigibles hovering in the sky above Africa and England and various points between.

The people of Nowhere Else were mildly surprised to wake up the next morning and find that a circus had suddenly appeared in the extensive grounds of Calendar House, but they didn't ask any questions. After all, you have to be pretty good at minding your own business to live in a place called Nowhere Else.

The man who took over the Whippersnapper flat at Blankstone Buildings has a son who is bigger and stronger than Zack Meaner. He also has eleven dogs. Mr. Meaner sneezed himself out the window and hit his head. When he woke up, he was a nicer person.

The Flying Gonzaloonies were delighted to see Petronella Patella and immediately became as meek as lambs. Petronella paid up her rent, retrieved the painting of Great Uncle Hinkley, and came back to Nowhere Else as comanager of the Circus of Wonder with Mom and Marcus. She spends her time these days keeping the Flying Gonzaloonies in order and looking after Antony Andrew Winterbottom, whom she married last year. They have a baby son named Garribaldi Patella-Winterbottom. Gary has two teeth and he bites.

Amanda Barton-Boote is very annoyed at being left out of all the excitement. She comes to stay at the circus every summer, and is currently planning a career as a ringmaster.

Timothy Whuffenpuffen-Whippersnapper is very happy. He now makes a point of calling Great Uncle Hinkley "You Old Wretch" three times a day before breakfast, just to prove a point.

Fergus McDaftie has retired and handed over the Whippersnapper documents to his great nephew, William McDaftie. William thinks they must be forgeries, so he's filed them away in a deed box and forgotten about them.

And Great Uncle Hinkley? Well, Antony Andrew Winterbottom reports that his employer *may* be making plans to come out of retirement and launch a new venture. He describes this venture as top secret and very hush-hush. Great Uncle Hinkley refuses to comment, so he must be planning something pretty outlandish.

Marcus can't wait to see what happens next.

TITLES IN THE SERIES